j. t. baka

a life's shell

two albums of lyrics

seasons of silence

shorts

another obituary

yes

it's true

I was born

ready

the game

some might

call it art

I call it

the heart's desire

born deranged

eyes are gateways

into the soul

so the saying goes

luckily I

don't have one

and so

yes

you are right

about what

I am missing

a point of view

so to speak

or

a world with a view

as some might say

blindness of the heart

another obituary

yes

I was

the knife

a word

slipping out

a word

slipping by

smelling

blood

a wound opening

unseen

an avalanche of sounds

of other words

pouring out

bleeding

until

another word

slipping out

until

another word

slipping by

cauterizing

the wound

closing it

until

another word

slipping out

until

another word

slipping by

smelling blood

opening a wound

drowning out

the world

in silence

and blood

wisdom of the dead

life's

always

a missed opportunity

but that's

all

we got

and that's

all

you will ever get

our dear friend

another obituary

he always

tried

so they

said

and yes

it's true

I did

the colour of snow

and all of a sudden

the master painted the silence

with a broad

but delicate stroke

of his bold brush of fate

winter in my heart

a landscape

sleeping under a blanket of snow

the sun

in a cloudless sky of intense blue

smiles upon it

a place

of peace and tranquility

in harmony with itself

a place

pure and virgin

and innocent

a place

of cold and breath-taking

overwhelming beauty

a place of awe

that's how

I pictured my love to you

a place too

cold and terrifying

to live in permanentely

a place

just for short visits

a place

most beautiful and alive

on pictures

or in memories

until you polluted it

with your presence

until you destroyed it

my utopia of my love to you

my refuge

I hate you

for it

but I am also thankful

you freed me

from my prison

you set me free

to love you

as you love me

charlene

true memories of lies

distance

looking back

at what once

was my life

I discover

something

something

funny and sad

at the same time

something

I would call

true memory of lies

oh nostalgia

before battle

standing on the porch

in the morning

watching east

I see the sun rising

and the sand of the desert

turning into a sea of ashes

standing on the porch

at noon

watching south

I see the sea of ashes

turning into an ocean of tears

standing on the porch

in the evening

watching west

I see the sun going down

and the ocean of tears

turning into a cosmos of the deepest blue

standing on the porch

at night

watching north

I see the cosmos all around

turning my hurting battle scars

into illuminated battle stars sky high

standing on the porch

in the morning

just before sunrise

I see the stars

floating gently

down to earth

like snow

touching my soul

rekindling my hope

restoring my love

for the one in the house

behind me

for the one

I left behind

when called to arms

for the one

I am going to face

for the first time

after the war

shadowed mirrors

following

the ashen trail of time

I came to a lake

at its shores

a mermaid awaited

me

smiling at her

I took a deep plunge

and dived

losing myself

in the depth

of her soul

while her eyes

mirrored the starlight

in the nightsky

while the stars

in the nightsky

mirrored the lights

in her eyes

smiling at me

she took a deep plunge

and dived

losing herself

in the depth

of my soul

while the lake

mirrored the moon

above us

while the moon

mirrored the lake

in front of us

until a dark shadow

fell upon us

blackening

all mirrors

swallowing

all light

around us

and looking

for a way

to snuff out

the light in us

until a turtle

sitting on a rock

near us

started to play

a bright tune

on its flute

at the light tune

the shadow caught fire

ignited in a burst

and burnt

inside out

so the light

was liberated

once again

and so our love

was freed

from its shakles

and so our fairy tale

got its

happy ending

after all

turtle

one day

I wanted

to treat my love

to something lovely

I asked

the turtle of my love

for advice

after deliberating

what would be best

it told me a recipe

for a mushroom soup

following

the turtle of my love

to the forrest

next to our home

for ingredients

I was walking

through the woods

getting lost

in the twilight

filtering through the branches

I found myself finally

in a field

full of mushroom clouds

with my head

in the clouds

I collected as much

as I could

happily

I followed

the turtle of my love

back to our home

I started to prepare

the mushroom soup

in the kitchen

right under

a woodblook print of a turtle

standing on a little island

in a pound

staring at the moon

high in the sky

staring into the pot

while stirring the soup

I caught my reflection

on the surface of the soup

discovering

I was the turtle of my love

I seasoned the soup

with all my love

for all seasons

for my love

to enjoy

true moments of lies

in revisiting

my life

I'm not reliving

my glories

I am rediscovering

my failures

but in doing so

I am also solving

a mystery

there are

true moments of lies

by this

I don't mean

that lies

creating their own realities

in which

of course

there are truth and lies

by this

I don't mean

that there are

honest lies

by this

I don't mean

that there are

true lies

by this

I mean

there is this moment

this very short moment

this blink of an eye

in which

a lie creates a truth

and while walking through it

lives in it

this moment

when the other person

believed in me

when I said

I love you

oh charlene

story of a house

<u>I</u>

a story

so they say

has a beginning

and a middle

and an end

sometimes

a story has

a beginning indeed

but no middle

and definitely no end

just like real life

sometimes

a story has

just an ending

but no beginning to start with

and no middle obviously

just like real life

and other times

there is only

the middle part

of a story

with no beginning

and no end at all

just a meaningless fragment

like most of real life is

but there are

also times

when a story

has to take everything

in its own hands

to get off the ground

to see it all through

from start to finish

to get over with itself

and move on

so

spot on

and

fire away

he didn't know

what happened

he didn't know

why it happened

he just knew

that it did

that she did

she happened

he saw her

and he knew

everything was good

he saw her

and he knew

they were meant to be

and they were

for the time being

III

it was not

his story

it was not

her story

it was

their story of happiness

until

she didn't know when

she didn't know how

she ended it

for herself

for him

for them

and for their children

that's how

it goes

that's how

it went

in their case at least

IV

the house

he built

on a foundation of ashes

the house

he built

with walls of fire

the house

he built

with a roof of smoke

the house

he built

through a blood sacrifice

the house

he supposedly built

as a home for his family

this house

turned into a pyre

for his dream of family life

this house

turned into a grave

for his wife

and children

a tragedy

for all involved

running in circles (black hole in hell)

following

your dream

you discover

you are

following

your star

until you

discover

the light

in front of you

is the bridge

you burned

before starting

on your quest

until you

discover

the light

in front of you

is the home

you set on fire

before starting

on your quest

until you

discover

the fires

you are caught

in between

are the borders of the hell

you put yourself into

by

extinguishing

your inner light

by

betraying

your dream

a way out

when the lies

turn out

not to be the lies

they were supposed

to be

when the truth

turns out

not to be the truth

it was supposed

to be

what are you

gonna do

then

what are you

looking for

then

anything else

but

anything else

way out

there

a lie's shell

hunting

of your dreams

in your screams

climbing

up the mountain

upside down

swimming

the waterfall

upriver

scooping out

a cloud

carving yourself out

of a woodblock

conquering the heart

of the heartless

turning the soul

of the soulless

loving

hate

hating

love

a toll of loniless

to be paid

for now

and for all of eternity

first blood.death metal

the undead immortal

fed up with his faked destiny

decided to grow up

to escape his deadborn fate

he didn't really know

what he was doing

he didn't really know

what he was up to

he thought

it would be a mere dance

with his shadow

he thought

it would be a mere flirt

with his mirror image

he didn't realize

he was a mere mirror image

he didn't realize

he was a mere shadow

until this very moment

when he tasted

death

for the very first time

and maybe

for the very last time

as well

let's see

what destiny

has in store for him

let's see

what his fate

will be

after death

proof

a life's shell is

a lie

a lie's shell is

a life

a life is

a lie

a lie is

a life

a life is

a shell

a lie is

a shell

a life is

a life

a lie is

a lie

a shell is

a shell

a life is

a lie is

a shell is

a lie is

a life is

just a play on words

a poem's fate

how to get

from *a* to *b*

it's easy

if you are in a river

just follow the flow

it's even easier

if you are staying in one place

doing nothing

time and gravity

will do the trick

so it's really easy

in real life

just follow your destiny

or let fate take over

and it's easy

in art too

it's easy

if you are in a movie

just follow the light

it's easy

if you are in a song

just follow the music

it's easy

if you are in a painting

just follow the strokes of the brush

and the same is true

if you are in a story

just follow the movement of the pen

but how

to get from *a* to *b*

if you are

the director

the composer

the painter

the writer

well

that's

another story

and

if your are destiny

if your are fate

that's another story

altogether

a story

for later

Credits *seasons of silence. shorts*

Written (analogue): 08.-19.01.2021.

Written (digital): 08.-19.01.2021.

Final mix: 22.01.2021.

Photography: Simon Wagenschütz.

Credits *charlene. true memories of lies*

Idea: 03.02.2021.

Written (analogue): 05.-14.02.2021.

Written (digital): 05.-16.02.2021.

Final mix: 17.02.2021.

Photography: Simon Wagenschütz.

Impressum

Redaktionsschluss: 28.02.2021.

Fotografien: Simon Wagenschütz.

©2021 baka, j. t.
Herstellung und Verlag: BoD - Books on Demand,
Norderstedt.

ISBN-13: 9783753426181.